poetry:

a

means

to

healing

# poetry:

## a

## means

## to

## healing

tami

## hasapopoulos

Luna Literary Press
Saint Paul, MN

Luna Literary Press, Saint Paul, MN

Library of Congress Control Number: 2025922503
Paperback ISBN: 979-8-9997995-0-0
eBook ISBN: 979-8-9997995-1-7
Book cover art and design by dedesign.eco
Interior design by Kate Huber-Parker
Editorial production by KN Literary Arts

May this book

remind me always

how strong

and worthy

I am.

# contents

# foreword

Tami is a gentle and wise soul whose unwavering passion for helping others live their best lives has captivated my heart. Through her dedicated healing practice and her nurturing of both her garden and spirit, she embodies the essence of a true lightworker—one who continuously amazes me with her peaceful, generous heart.

Our friendship, built over countless Zoom calls spanning continents and time zones, is a testament to the power of genuine connection. We've shared both joys and sorrows, even when months pass between conversations or when life's challenges keep us apart. A bond that holds steady and strong.

This book is a powerful testament to who she is. It is raw, honest, and deeply moving—a reflection of everything she has lived through and risen from. In these pages, she finds her voice and speaks her truth with courage and grace. It is more than poetry—it is the heart of an extraordinary human being laid bare.

—*Mona Lerch*,
creative director & CEO
Women United ART MOVEMENT
womenunitedartmovement.com

# letting go

realized

grieved

*r e s t*

healed

freedom

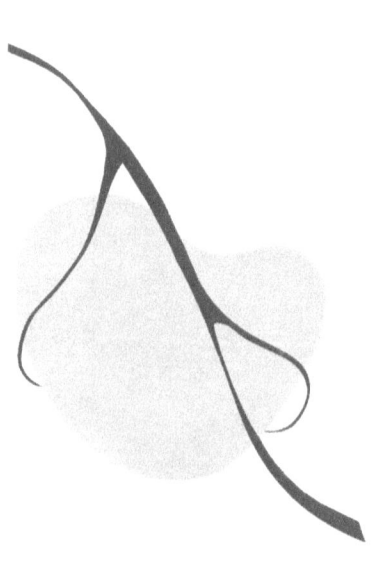

fire

# loneliness

lack of love
a hollowed heart
how to break free

what is love

*L-O-V-E*
how to receive whom to believe
is it love if you are not able
to show it grow it sow it give it away freely

one-dimensional what does it mean lonely

*L-O-V-E*
aching heart breaking apart
does love really exist if you're not able
to see it hear it feel it

*L-O-V-E*
seeking a love overflowing
instead feeling emptiness
longing

lonely

# shattered

spirit crushed
light is dimmed
joy slowly fades

believe in and hold on to yourself
love and fight for yourself
do not succumb you are strong

*mind body soul*

*freedom*

# abandoned

excruciating pain invading
rejection piercing

unseen crevices

heart is breaking

broken pieces heaping
shattered dreams escaping

sea of loneliness

drowning in aching

breathe in calm
body swells light fills

nature soothes
sunshine holds
wind blows a gentle touch

reminiscence i am not lost

# laundry

let me be clear

it was not about the laundry

it is never about the laundry

mountains reaching the sky

vast and wide echoing cries

aching emptiness burning a (w)hole inside

it will erupt without a sigh

laundry not laundry then why

*emptiness loneliness longing*

# frustration

so
much
to
say

bottled away

where are the words

stuck in my throat

*why* can't they hear

nonsense escapes

# absolve

seriousness taken too far
a heart lacking in lightness
not playful or free
holding grudges not meant for me

but wait
what could we be
what should we be

*a b s o l v e   l - o - v - e*

laughter
conversation
connecting

liberating

so many things bring us together
in a world that only we can see
whimsical fantasy brought to reality

freedom to roam
safe in soul
a place of our own nobody knows

free to be

free
to
*absolve*

# serial (soul killer) career

chosen for her at age twelve

a nightmare a slow tortuous death
kidnapped innocence stolen for the pleasure
of many dark empty souls

a choice to be complicit (porn)

normalized in society
accessed freely
awareness necessary

rescue her
S T O P the insanity
put them out of business

E N D complicity (porn)

# wounding

laughter fades
joy evades
light goes out
nothing   nothing   nothing
wounding

a giant monster scheming under your bed
keeps you fearful
bewilders your mind
devouring life bringing dread

not asked for but doled out
time after time

the wounded wound
a cycle goes on
who's gonna stop it

perpetual predator
dangerous to ignore

you cannot hide
it chips at your psyche
you look for a way
grasping not finding

will you survive
wait
that is all you know

survival

tattered and torn wishing for more
seeking answers
a way to break free

emptiness growing
shrinking away
losing steam
hazy gaze
grip is slipping sliding away
floating floating drifting drifting

eyes close
shutting down
wounding wounding frown frown frown
dangling by a string shrinking
drowning in grief sinking
devastating uncertainty
family of fear
nowhere to go
emptiness sown

eventually sleep soothes
bestows rest to the soul

i will not let wounding win
sometimes i get tired
the battle is big lonely

everyone around is wounded too
conversation tainted by a wounded lens

trust is broken
intuition dulled
dark forces surround
discernment prevented

truth becomes diluted
submission the mission
wounding wins

the fight is difficult long
got to keep strong
courage mustered
the battle *MUST* be won

i will stand i will love
wounding will not overcome
dark forces are weak when we speak

a door opens light shines in giving us strength
hope for future sidles in
heart fills creativity floods

make a pact join hands reflect
you are going to win
it is all good for now a sigh of relief residing

rest   rest   rest

i will not be alone

RISE UP

dark forces will cower when we rise together

believe in the truth found within
shut out the noise go inside
nurture the connection meant to thrive
the gift of intuition compassion and life

strength is yours confidence to share
the battle fades the masses raise we are one

praise

purity love compassion remain
souls are mended geysers of pain
wounding ended

praise

gaze toward the sun wounding overcome
the battle is won

love and light endure must be aware on guard
preserving

laughter fades
joy evades
light goes out

nothing

n o t h i n g

n  o  t  h  i  n  g

wounding

# disavow

pain intentionally inflicted
embedded deeply in my soul

over and over the behavior continues
layers upon layers glued together

a sliver deep in the heart causes aching

over time the pain becomes debilitating

cannot be ignored i begin to mourn

words surface to explain the devastating pain

unlocking the dam of feelings

releasing the burden held in my being

hoping for acknowledgment

apology

nevertheless i choose to let go for my soul
my personal freedom

escape the source end the pain

begin to trust my virtue again

# generational trauma

tears dry up
anger rises

grateful for the direction He gives

clarity
support
guidance

healing encourages

it is safe to let go of the pain
time to live gain conviction

the battle begins

righteous indignation
standing firm
bravery comes from spirit
light paves the way

break the strongholds of the souls
protect the innocent ones to come

conquer trauma make way for generations of
inner peace and solace

# purgatory

tears roll like thunder
welling up and spilling
down the hills of your cheeks

heart is broken
when words are spoken
but not understood

unable to penetrate
the fortress
hiding another's emotional pain

agony
frustration
anguish

casualty of another's fragmented
pieces

a block wall
unable to access

expression meant to expand understanding
ears unable to hear
perception veiled in past recollection
negative energy guiding thoughts and vision

lost in a battle of past identity
seeing faces
hearing voices not speaking presently

how to get through
a fortress a wall
the blocks are too tall

damage reaches wide
corrosive explosive destructive

walls can be sanctuaries
or
dungeons of purgatory

protection needed
from fragmented pieces

ridged in thinking
steeped in stagnation

break down the wall

choose to heal
create a window
into your soul

end the hostility
suffering
heartbreak and misery

# betrayal

a sensitive being an easy target punching bag
dumping ground

betrayal of trust not a reflection of you

make room for who you once were
before the betrayal left you wearied and vacant

muster the strength

fight to access *who you are*

reach for the light that surrounds and holds
you tight

don't give up or lose your ground

the soul knows the truth and never abandons

rise up to shine your light on a new canvas

# a ravaged heart

a heart steeped in rejection manipulation
misuse of truth

floating in a sea of diminished integrity

will the heart heal
i cannot tell
nothing seems real
words words words
what do they really reveal

only the universe knows

my soul will disclose

i unflinchingly listen

# exhaustion

giving your all not wanting to fall

unable to see the top
the mountain so tall
inch by inch is it enough

the path is narrow
how will we cross
hope for a widening

each new day brings optimism

path closes
now what
a wearing down

time to gear up
try again
oh dear

is it worth the journey
look for the signs
insight will tell

a mountain cannot detour
courage strength fierceness for family

# unloved

all you ever wanted was to love

a heart that cares never hateful but despised

the more you reach the further love lies

your only desire is love and connection

but living with loneliness and deception

existing in a world where you are
misunderstood avoided and barely tolerated

sadness overcomes you want to run
unbearable pain you are drifting away
no destination

tell me

why do you deserve to be so unloved
what have you done
but want nothing more than the best
for the ones you love

why is it that strangers welcome you
with appreciation easy conversation
no averted eyes bored or annoyed glances

while receiving your ideas and information
no judgment and indignation

your reality a nightmare full of despair

while nighttime brings comfort
dreams bring life
no misunderstanding or strife

an experience of quiet restful peace
where your heart is calm hurt by no one

lonely soul in a world where you do not belong
where those you chose do not care
and heartache permeates the air

ignored despised cast aside
condemnation expressed throughout your life

tell me again
why do you deserve to be so unloved

# out of the shadows

woven together by the Creator
made perfectly
for who you were meant to be

threads unraveled
to suit someone else's comfort and ease
suppressed beauty

hide pieces of yourself
accept repression the message
conform to society

shadows hold the stories
of tales told by wounded souls

falsehoods dimmed your vivacity

shadows darkened as you grew
believing the stories told to you

projected fear anger distress
robbed you of personality
step out of the shadows
liberate from oppression

retell your stories

realize
your intrinsic
creativity

# the end

the heart no longer breaks
emotions stop flowing
emptiness ceases to ache

the fight left the heart drained and hollow

is it the end

the past is complex
confusion overwhelms was it pretending
a fairytale life

dreams drifting out of reach
do we let them slip away let them go

now is time to rest the soul
begin the healing from within
resist temptation to control

no one knows from here
where we go

# stepping up

why have i allowed them to compel me
to question my integrity my philosophy
my sensibility

i wavered in my confidence my purpose

none of this making sense to me

why have i allowed myself to step aside

it is time to take back what i have given away

i am making space
drowning out the voices
that segment me fulfilling my destiny

i will no longer quiet my voice
play small or hide

i am created to fly to embrace my mind
to share wide

let it be known
you will not recognize me as a clone
get ready to have your mind blown
it is true i do have a mind of my own

# disenchanted

lied to
thinking you know
only seeing the surface
hidden below a betrayal of soul

little by little subtle innuendo
meant to disempower
slowly *d e s t r o y* you

possessing a heart
unable to comprehend
activity of sin
by someone professing love and devotion

messing with your mind
twisting it around
insanity in motion

connection is strong with the heavens above

showing you truths when you least expect it

arming you
with strength courage and fierceness

anger guarding your heart not the solution
overcoming the beast is your mission
sparing the innocent a life of submission

# mental hellness

encircled by energies meant to drain

truths unraveling deceit explained

look to soul for strengthening

repel the wounds not meant for you

embrace your light

heart protected

strength renewed

mental wellness

# the effort is futile

filling someone else's empty vessel
will leave you emptying your own
little by little slowly killing your soul

piece by piece your heart breaks apart
rescuing a soul is not your role
especially when they are resentful

it begins well-intentioned
then you find yourself
in a sea of deception
questioning how did this happen
blaming yourself for decades of abuse

until the day of reckoning the awakening
you are finally able to name your pain
it is your right to heal and to live
you have so much to give

the world is filled with people who steal
your role is to learn and to heal

enable yourself to move on

with the realization

your potential sparks greatness

in those you attract

so show yourself and enjoy the reveal

# never apologize

for faith

for caring

for feeling

for resting

for healing

for believing

for fearlessness

for speaking truth

for being different

for being imperfect

for meeting your needs

for establishing routines

for avoiding toxic people

for being kindly assertive

for being highly informed

for taking care of yourself

for possessing confidence

for going against the grain

for establishing boundaries

for avoiding toxic situations

for not compromising your safety

for practicing a new way of being

never apologize

for working toward your healed self

for choosing to live a sacred meaningful life

# a spark that ignites

a long and arduous journey
left me worn and full of longing

enlightenment leads the way
as i become empowered to apply
comfort and care necessary to break free
from psychological injury

renewed strength curiosity capacity

a birthing

excitement for possibility

at last a life without squashing

my spirit is unleashed to set me free

a spark that ignites glows up a life
meant to be a vessel
of compassion and peace

# i am peace

i am peace
i am grounded
i am steeped in faith

but make no mistake
i will show my fierceness when it is needed

i am resilient
i am strong
i have endured monsters

do not come against me

for i am steady
i have ancestors behind me
angels to guide me

i see i know i am not fearful
you are merely a shadow
i call in the light that exposes

darkness dispels
i am victorious

# the power of sisterhood

the wild feminine rises
when we seek to heal our soul
when we believe in our unique gifts
and trust our intuition

seeking the support of our sisters
plays a vital role in obtaining
the unbridled power of feminine spirit

we embody that sacred energy
a spiritual force of creativity
inspiring answers through the fluidity
of intuition and feelings

we are powerful creators communicators
matched with our masculine
we are invincible

the very characteristics we need
to achieve the fulfillment we seek
come from our own power
and from our sisters spanning all ages

we achieve by gleaning experience
support love and wisdom
sourced from the feminine archetypes

the mother the lover the huntress
the sage the maiden the mystic
the queen

develop the wholeness
it takes for her to be seen
to be guided to greatness
not just for her but for the greater

sisterhood brings light
as we pour into one another
we rise together
making way for the advent of a new brilliance

the gift and power of sisterhood bind us
together we embark on a journey
to bring truth that heals

# the time has come

leave behind what was
memories are all they are

a realization that leaves a dark mark
on my heart

moving on will be hard

a realization there is no love
there never was

i entered a void that would mar my heart
fill it with sorrow

i am not as strong as i thought
i endured too much for far too long

a heart can only ache in silence
for the sake of love

sometimes you have to sacrifice
for a benevolent reason

i will not fall prey to a demon

# my greatest warrior

my body my warrior
had it not been for my body
i would not have survived
the darkest of times

once i learned what healed
i fed my body abundantly
my mind and symptoms cleared
my thoughts were loving and dear
i began to see the truth
become more aware

the power of darkness
slithers in stealthily
sometimes it comes in packages
wrapped beautifully

be careful of words
that are not congruent
behaviors that seem loving
but then contradict
trust your intuition
you are not crazy

the strength and the fortitude
my body gifted
pulled me from the chains that bound me
i was able to break free
to see everything clearly

lightness clarity confidence in truth
were just some of the fruits
my body afforded me

my connection strengthened
with the light that surrounds
nature spoke soothed and healed me

my intuition sharpened
as i cared for my body
gifting me protection
from the trap of deception

thank you to my body for fighting for me
my warrior i am free

# subtle horrors

withholding affection and connection
driving me to question my worth

subtle innuendo meant to devalue

consistent twisting of truth
leading to a state of confusion
loneliness despair

how is this fair

my soul experiencing decades
trying to build a life with a narcissist
actually fortified my faith

the mountain of strength i would need
the courage i would have to summon
to escape the covert abuse
that no one will ever see
no matter to me the veil has been lifted

the end is near
i will endure coming out secure
in knowing exactly who i am
never to be manipulated again

i will use this experience to support
and to love those who fall prey
to the insidious monsters
of emptiness and darkness

# self-assurance

we are innately more powerful
more resourceful
than the men who made the rules

forge your own path
listen to your intuition
foster and nurture your creativity
trust your rules and guidelines
no one knows you like you do

those who are uncomfortable
with your decisions are uncomfortable
with what is living deep inside them

it is not our responsibility to comfort
stay in your alignment

do not give in to doubt
stand firm in your wholeness
you earned it

# in the face of conflict

ask yourself
where does your anger originate
have you been silenced, ignored
are you in a space of danger
is there an unknown
is your confidence low
do you feel alone

you have the power
to use your voice
out loud
in a letter
or with a mediator

your feelings are real
no matter if validated
express your truth
it will gift you self-value

if your truth is not received
it is for you

keep using your voice
it is your choice
until you find a safe way
to exercise your agency

acceptance we cannot control
thoughts actions and emotions
of another soul

gives us the gift of self-control
and releases us of responsibility
a problem that is not ours to solve

refrain from giving your power away
it only leads to frustration confusion
and the illusion of insanity

there is no way to know what pain
lies in a troubled soul
unless they open the door

as we embody self-regulation
we can accept the responsibility
to self-love and self-correct
protecting ourselves during conflict

# to all women and girls

it is not the knight in shining armor

it is not the prince or the king

it is the horse that possesses
the power strength and ability

it is the horse that holds you safe
as you are highly positioned
while gliding through life

the horse is the one
who establishes and maintains
a connection like no other

it is the horse who shows you
who you are
allowing you to discover

the horse is the one
who draws you to healing
who teaches you to be strong
as you claim your power

it is the horse who teaches you
to communicate to assert yourself
gently
compassionately

it is with the horse
you will forge
an everlasting bond

the horse will accept you
despite a flaw
remaining faithful
without end

the horse
provides
the safest relationship
of all

# forgive me

waves of emotion explode
tears splash from my eyes
sobbing erupts
from the depths of my gut
overwhelmed with self-love
my throat tightens up

i barely catch my breath
i know where you have been

the rocky terrain valleys so low
you did not see
you were meant
to encounter safety and peace
after years of torment

you possess strength
a heart of gold
a light as bright as the moon

forgive me
for keeping you hidden
i will shed the cocoon
spread my wings
reveal my colors
for it is safe to be seen

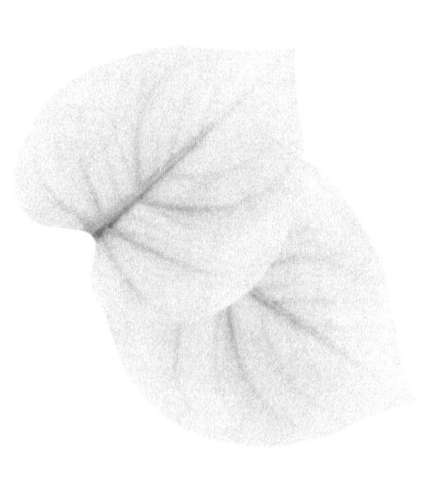

earth

# wisdom of nature

the world likes to show us the worst
coerces us into believing the lies
submerging us into sadness

the age-old battle of good versus madness

we prevail by recognizing
a sense of resonance
with nature that exists for us

breathe deep into your being
release all the lies
experience the truth that nature reveals

earthly mother holds us steady

sun embraces with warmth and healing

birds sing to soothe lifting the spirit

rivers wash away renew

trees maintain stability through roots
anchored deep in the earth
they lose their leaves but stand tall
till they return

snow blankets
bringing rest
until a new season begins

rain satisfies a thirst
ushering in new growth

creatures never worry but trust
there will be enough

nature instills truth

we are resilient

# sweatshirt & sweatpants

the absence of
connection
intimacy
warmth

an unlikely replacement
hugging my body
comfort exists
snugness

a reminder of love

a laid-back vibe
*gentleness*
freedom to move
*never constrained*
playfulness attained

# magnetized

spiraling into the depths
of the pools of a digital world
drowning a virtual death

building a life in your device

*come up for air*

reality stares

*i am here    i am here    i am here*

# planet earth

not an easy place to thrive

dark forces temptation greed
insanity galore
ignored

bodies poisoned
brains clouded
manipulation

wake up to restoration
breathe in light begin anew
tend to earth
tend to you

take a stand
grow together
clean clear heal within
fruits vegetables herbs spices
chose the wild over vices

we are nature one with earth
no more manufactured
food from mother *(earth)*
meant to nurture

rise together
stop the fall
we are earth one and all

heed intuition
fill your body
with what it desires
fruit from earth
meant to energize and inspire

your body cries out
no more numbing life-destroying poison

choose self-control
over letting them control

end the madness see the truth
health is wealth rich is soul
protect nurture witness
we are nature not made
we have purpose strength and power

humanity step away
from easy fast and nonnutritious
we are precious and worth every effort

your body your choice
earth to body we thrive
manufactured to body we suffer

tend to the earth
receive from the earthly mother
we are A L I V E

# rushing

what is the point
where is the end

why are you rushing

who cares

to what end

what is the reward

stress
anxiety
frustration and more

slow down

look around

breathe in

ground

# petals

we are born a flower
brimming with petals

unique qualities characteristics
given only to us

supple
tender
delicate

with nourishment care light
our petals flourish with delight

when acknowledged
we bloom

our petals grow vibrant
with all our colors

like a flower we stand tall toward the sun

as time goes on
words have power to make us strong

but when spoken to us with scorn
our petals fall
one by one

plucking the petals from the stem
robs the beauty from within

careless words actions too
wither our blooms
sapping our vitality

soon the stem becomes
lifeless

petals wilt

# gardening

seeds to be sown
planted beneath the surface
growing roots deep and wide

the purpose
life

joy
beauty
fruitfulness

a slow gentle process
warmth watering light

growth is tender trusting

every day excitement and wonder

each season bringing change
gifts we cannot measure
seeds sown deep within

giving life
a treasure

# biophilia

we are conditioned
to rely on man-made
remedies and cures

unnatural far from how our bodies
operate
communicate
restore

we are nature
meant to coexist
there is no denying nature's power

consistent interaction with nature
a blessing
a healing reaction

why the disconnection

venture out of man-made cages
that stifle creation
and partner with the vibration

achieve a peace your body craves
nature in all its glory
waiting for you to participate
as you satisfy your tendency
to harness earth intelligence

alleviate
physical and psychological imbalance

# internal power

power received from above
resides within
easy access if you seek
close your eyes call it in
feel the peace

cleanse the body
free up space
confusion clears
the mind expands

our brain is our power
the motherboard
the information system

don't take it for granted protect it
be wary of losing your guide
through experimentation

electricity in the brain
needs no enhancement
it is the outside world that inhibits
shadows dampen your intuition

our brains are capable of wonder
wisdom discovery exploration
depth expansion the potential power
of transmission pathways are endless

explore the regions of mystery
without numbing or mind-altering
mechanisms

the answer is in the cleansing

you have three homes
the earth the mind the body

healing our mission

nurture and nourish with wild foods
fruits vegetables herbs spices

deprivation of troublemakers to gain protection

drown out the noise meant to confuse
and elicit fear

searching for answers
where answers mislead
lessen the connection behind our eyes

embrace a brightness that fills your head
diminishing darkness making room
for enlightenment

instead of blocking resisting and mocking
let your mind expand beyond your horizons

imagine a mind limitless and unbridled
moving with ease pressures cease

feed the electricity needed
from fruits to sustain the brain highways

don't give in to the endless song
that sings that protein is the end all
let that sweet serenity bring peace

creativity

# escape

escaping the pain of invisibility
the constant manipulation of vulnerability
fleeing from imposed insecurity
to a space of peace and safety

# birdsong

birdsong pierces the early morning shadows

music to my ears unburdening my soul

my heart overflows with emotion

a string of sweet melodies dancing with me

taking me to faraway spaces

indescribably free

a soul tethered not astray

a beautiful way to begin a day

# rain

ominous dark grey clouds
blanket the sky

evergreen branches
dance in the wind

crystalline droplets
a soothing staccato rhythm

through a window watching the show
i feel the boom of thunder as it rumbles

rain streaks the window like the tears
of my soul

thunder somehow makes me feel less alone

i am comforted by the rhythm of rain
and surrounding trees leafless

lightning slices the sky
i anticipate another boom

the excitement and wonder as i imagine
God is whispering to me
as i drift off to sleep peacefully

upon awakening
the little green leaves appear on the trees

the miracle of nature is astonishing

# a reminder to myself

i am not normal or ordinary

*i am extraordinary*

i am not hateful

*i am compassionate*

*i am empathetic*

*i am encouraging*

*i am agreeable*

*i am generous*

*i am helpful*

*i am loving*

i am not judgmental

*i am discerning*

*i am curious*

*i am accepting*

*i am open-minded*

i am not doom and gloom

*i am aware*

*i am informed*

*i see what is possible*

*i will not settle for less*

*i offer solutions*

i am not negative

*i am realistic*

*i see joy in simplicity*

i am approachable

*i am friendly*

*i am welcoming*

*i am easy to talk to*

*i would never undermine relationships*

*or others' well-being*

i am not normal or ordinary

i am extraordinary

# wheel of numbers

time
tick tock watch the clock
nine to five is all we got

never enough time to get it all done
exhausted and frazzled no time for fun

busy is revered slow and steady dishonored
chasing time becomes embedded (a way of life)
trapped in a wheel where are we headed

hop off it is an illusion

time is of the essence emphasizes
deadlines

time should be about presence
lifelines

a place to be a place to go
notice the little things
be purposeful

overlooking the seconds
we miss the gems
the meaningful moments for reflection

riches are in stillness

savor the journey

rushing to the next disregards our
achievements

joy comes in the slow exhale
no need to chase

time is sufficient

# simple serenity

serenity
does not have to be
something we wait for

serenity is something we create
in the moment
sometimes in the mind

we create the feeling
when circumstances seem bleak
and chaos abounds

keeping it simple
may be all we need
to achieve the serenity we seek

a hug can make all the difference
providing you with warmth love
and affection

from someone you feel attuned to
someone who sees all parts of you

if the luxury of the hug is unavailable
nature is my go-to

using my breath
i pull air deep into my core

using my mind's eye
i observe the qualities
that define serenity for me

i call them in

my favorite
recalling my experiences in nature

nature provides me what i love
by engaging my senses

my awareness attunes
to the benefits nature offers

to ease my mind
fill my heart
and set my soul free

serenity is all in your perception

you get to choose
how you view life
and embody the reflection

your mind is powerful
you are in control

exercise your mind
serenity will follow

# choose

choice is a right
choice is freedom
choice empowers
choice is necessary
choice can validate
choice can alienate
choice is a privilege
choice takes resolve
choice takes courage
choice can be difficult
choice can be heartbreaking
choice takes time to feel right
choice can leave you uncertain

a choice can take time before you experience
the benefits of making it

you must choose or you will never know

# play love laugh dance

imagine a space where the motivation
for control never exists

we are for each other

individuality is admired
gifts are allowed to flourish
no one person is better than the other

a space that honors support
the golden ring is community

a space where we are encouraged
to play love laugh dance

let us strive for this

# clearing

i am entranced by the lilting of birds
excited by the arrival of spring

the breeze moving trees harmoniously

i imagine twigs laden with leaves
sweeping away unsettling memories
from my brain

clearing debris from years of gaslighting

a breath of new life my future is bright

i am living

# remembering me

i miss you
where did you go
i long to find you
you were silly full of laughter
wild and free

take as much time
and space as you need
healing is not to be rushed
especially when you are dealing
with one thousand cuts

you have pored over the wounds
thinking they were healed
as your awareness grows
the deeper layers demand to be seen
crying out for tenderness and love
only you can minister

you have created safety
that satisfies the craving
for the compassion you deserve

extend the same devotion
you lovingly gifted to ease suffering
as an essential key to dissolving
your own agony

the echoes of trauma
drumming in your mind
fail to confine as truth flows
like a river rolling over the stones
softening the edges

i am with you on this journey to the sea
together we will celebrate
the ebb and the flow

through your painstaking diligence
and unwavering commitment to rise up
i recognize me emerging and expanding

the consistent tearing down
takes strength to rebuild
thank you for not cracking

together we are stepping into
our beautiful energy

water

# a collection of poems

in no particular order poured onto the page
my psyche chose to release in words

a series of sacred profound feelings
a necessary path to healing

i am grateful for these pages

a witness to my burdens an offer
of compassion written solace
and a source of connection

# eyes wide open

do you see

pain and suffering

beauty of the universe

slow intentional living loving existing

quiet breathing quiet thinking

feeling
crying
seeking

*hanging on*

*healing*

# harmony

this world
a lonely valley
emptiness abounds

lessons to be learned
—not a playground

*If only* we collectively attained
complete understanding
cavernous hearts would peak

*maybe*
*just*
*maybe*

life wouldn't be so bleak

harmony

# self-connection

a space where you begin
and the world ends

free from the haunting
of past stories
created with a lack of wisdom
and understanding

a safe place where all parts of you
are welcomed and accepted

here you have access to those parts
that were hidden away

where curiosity and wonder take place
this is where the healing happens

a place where you choose
a place where you open the door
to envision and explore

experience joy of getting to know you
nurture a new relationship with you

replace those past stories
with an autobiography

you *are* the author

# comfort in healing

trust your body
it knows how to heal
practice appreciation
for bodily systems
operating in synergy

patience is necessary
consistency is key
listen to the messages
your body communicates constantly

in stillness you can hear the melody
of a body system gently humming
there is comfort in the pulsing

as your body regulates
feel the connection
there is an awakening
to your God-given right to healing

# watermelon days

the crack
as i slide a knife into a watermelon
satisfies

an instant aroma of summertime
wafts toward my nose
reminding me of my childhood

that little girl sitting crossed-legged
in the fresh-cut summer grass
holding a deep-pink wedge
between her hands

her tastebuds engulfed
by the juicy sweetness
drowning out any concerns

she is fully immersed
in the joy of sunshine
as the watermelon juice
drips down her chest
painting her little white tee

cracking open that beautiful melon
i notice the curly stem
where the fruit was attached to the vine

i think to myself
it resembles a cord
connecting a child to her mother

at that moment i am reminded
that i too am connected
to the earthly mother

i am held i am loved i am connected

no longer
do i let the juice of the watermelon
drip down my chest
instead i choose to savor
each beautiful drop
while i embrace that lost little girl

# simple ritual

uncomplicated

life-giving ritual

peeled me from my bed

prevented me reliving the dread

numb acceptance

my efforts only fanned his fires

dragging myself to the cutting board
my only connection to existence

suffice it to say a lemon a knife
is all i could manage

sour juice a big glass of water
somehow opened my eyes
to a new frame of mind

one step
in the right direction
something to grasp

allowed me to incrementally
achieve the next level

the thirst i was quenching

a desire to reclaim my identity

the rest of the story my destiny

# soul sisters

on an island far from me
the universe gathered a group of women

homes scattered across the globe
we never would have met

our backgrounds diverse
a wide range of ages
differing race ethnicity culture
religious beliefs

each a feminine archetype
i would require
curated to hold space for me

i unknowingly
embarked upon a journey
to heal the pieces that kept me in survival

peeling away layers
of deep emotional pain
each one healed only to expose
more terrain

little did these women know
that just by their being
my heart would be full

i am eternally grateful to the four
the lover
the huntress
the mystic
the maiden

each one uniquely special
placed on my path
to lead me to the me
i was created to be

# something to ponder

i find value in saying no
there is an epidemic of people-pleasing
it is easy to get caught up in the status quo

living in an era where it is not welcome
to think for yourself the pressure is real
to follow the comfortable path
where you are guaranteed success

what if ego and fear were not so prevalent
i wonder if our choices would be different

is there only one version of success
i believe this is something to consider

would we be more grounded
interesting and less exhausted
if we explored the paths that allowed
our instincts to flow naturally
if we pursued the things that came easily

what if our choices ignite and inspire us
to share our passions daily

would our vacations feel different
if we did not feel the need
to escape our professions

# words

a beautiful tool
easy to use

can be soothing or scathing
expressive demeaning
provide direction and learning
clear up misunderstanding

beautiful words glow with

introspection
compassion
meaning

words have the power to foster
limitless healing

# an apology (to niko)

my heart breaks for the pain i have inflicted
no intention but injury occurred

wisdom without words
destroyer of trust
broken connection

damage requires restoration

you are pure love gifted from above
meant to be nurtured protected

no more broken hearts

please forgive me
i promise to evolve

i am filled with gratitude
for an apology accepted

i am devoted to communication
connection and healing
no more hiding words or feelings

# once upon a time

once upon a time
you were a baby
for a brief moment you were all mine

pure joy all through the days
and into the evenings

silly games played
stories made
adventures and escapades

my love for you knows no bounds
you are grown and dear to me
a gift i gratefully receive

treasure the memories
imagine and don't forget to play play play

love shared
hearts mended
independence achieved

you are ready
you are brave
spread your wings
realize your dreams

# an apology (to jake)

there are so many things
i have done wrong

inflicted pain
suffering too

hurt your heart
confused and frustrated you

never deserving but served

i apologize with my whole being
i vow to make it right
spending the rest of my time
offering healing

you are a soul of love light and wisdom
full of compassion deserving of nurturing
and protection

no more words unsaid
communication and action to be had
heart and soul preserved from harm
i solemnly promise to mend

my intention
you develop a knowing deep within
you are cherished

# gifts from my children

day to day a world of imagination
and play

purest unconditional love
no restrictions judgments
expectations only acceptance

no concerns free expression
creative play revived my inner child

access to pure joy and laughter

untouched by worldly sin
unconcerned by others' views
hang-ups not participating in
simply guided by the spirit within

life is weird and wonderful
making sense of it impossible

staying true to you is key
ignore the voices meant to dim
advice i would have given
to the little one within

it is not too late just more difficult
to navigate

one moment of your pure identity
gives you confidence clarity
and serenity

dissolving the lies of the past
brings light that outshines shadows

i am grateful for the experience
of innocence

break the chains that hold you back
allow that inner child to shine again

# a holy vow

i vow to myself never to carry
another soul's wounds

in my hallowed halls
i am safe to unpack the truths
i have kept from myself
and the lies
i have told myself
to protect my survival

i am crafting a gentle rhythm
of calm strength and wisdom
within a life of safety and presence

i am wrecking the survival toolshed
it is no longer needed

# me

i breathe deeply into my body

filling my lungs to their full measure

as i release the breath
cobwebs of sadness dissipate

tears flow from my eyes
cleansing decades of heartache

disconnected pieces are coming together

after a life of searching and searching
i am realizing the trust lies within me

i am the one who loves me
unconditionally and completely

it is me who has the capacity
to provide safety

it is me who will fulfill my deepest dreams
and my fullest destiny

no more searching
because i have come home

to me

# talking stick

summoning the talking stick
following a long-awaited respite
from a suppressed spirit

pouring forth wisdom from a soul
weary from a long spell of neglect
quelled

shaken awake by a thunderous quake
the vibration too sacred to mistake

the path is paved a golden weave
built to carry my feet to places
of sweet beginnings

i have earned a seat at the table
it is my turn to create a stable space
of change meant to heal as it reveals
a tale of truth

i walk forward in step with the one
who promises direction and guidance
toward heart fullness and freedom

# new beginning

a blanket of snow
preserving of soul
hibernation of healing

*r e s t i n g*

*r e s t o r i n g*

a period of reviving
creating *s p a c e* and *f l o w*

shed the old
make room for growth
wounds and pain melt away

seasons change
a new generation emerges
sprouting new patterns
that foster healthy souls

# coming out of hiding

lost in others' perceptions

watching listening learning

how should i be for them to accept me

am i not enough

conformity whose idea was this anyway

we are meant to possess our own identity

i will not be punished
for what you are afraid of
or what you do not understand

the more i adapt the more invisible i am

i assume that was the goal
to shrink my soul

thank you God for reminding me

you see something in me
that needs to be seen

i am coming out of hiding

# liberation

tangled in oppressive forces
free to be me finally

discovery of me
creatively precious me

my soul achieved sovereignty
connecting to the energy that is me

breathing in all life love destiny
a deliverance from sorrow and suffering

*liberating*

# poetry

a means to healing
a compassionate witnessing

freedom of speech
saying all offending none

bottled up feelings unable to speak
freed by letters on a sheet
release the suffering

no need for understanding

feelings flowing freely
a means to healing

poetry a prayer

# survival

it is my turn little one
you served me well
i needed it then
thank you for your protection

i see in you the strength the courage
i am in awe of all you experienced
and survived

you salvaged the song in my heart
the smile in my eyes
my capacity for empathy
and compassion

you can rest little girl
i got this now
you served me well

# deserving

*r e s t*

enough said

air

# home is in me

in my soul

a sanctuary

a vast expanse of ease
blankets me

i dance like a flickering fire
in the moonlight

i am the cup of tea

freedom to be me
oh the beauty

# information overload

consume my mind

fill the room

squeeze my head my chest

trapped in rhetoric

*my breath*
*my breath*
*my breath*

fill me with *spirit*

moon   stars   earth   trees

sunshine hugs me

i am at peace

# whisper

a gentle caress
a kiss for the soul

a lullaby freeing the mind
stirring the heart

eyelashes heavy
body resting

compassion received
free to sleep

# stranger

news
turmoil
darkness
i am petrified

walking fast feeling numb
where am i going but to no one
alone doom is looming

a stranger's hand
no voice no face
just a gentle warm embrace
enveloping my hand

a rush of warm light flooding

compassion

hand to hand soul to soul grateful

# searching

light exists

where to find it

searching heart defines it
soul survives by it
mind defies it

light surrounds us

use your voice cry out

light light light light light light light

it exists you cannot deny it

# those who know

locked in a box unable to breathe
consumed with pain unruly emotions
extinguish the hellish fires in me

solitude

no control
not finding a way
will i maintain

eyes closed tears escaping

the rescue of an open window
along comes the feeling
cool air swirling like a magical mist

deep in my nose bringing spring
a new me
cooling my brain
widening my perspective

finally feeling a sense of direction
easing the agony new perception

an ocean of air lifting me from the depths
of despair it becomes clear

i cannot be broken

at last a life of peace chosen

# angels

angels surround lift and support me
while whispering the words i need to hear

angels hold my hand letting me know
they are near as i find my strength
to let go of fear

i sense a lightness a space in my soul
a release what was destined to go

# not alone

believing i could fix it if only i did this
or did not do that it would all work out

possessing the mindset that anything
can be worked through until
i was trampled by truth

the life i fought to keep together
was a solitary endeavor

honesty and truth
were never part of the promise
leaving me alone in a union

i deserve more in life
than this heaviness in my chest

drying my eyes i reach for the sky
begging for sight
i know i am more
than what is tearing at my sanity

bolstered by the unseen
beyond the sky beyond the stars
a part of me unscarred

i find myself between the sun and moon
—illumination calling my name

exposing my vulnerability
i feel the pull of the moon
a wounding begins to flee my soul

i am not alone
but supported loved and held

i am safe
i am strong
i am guided

i realize i am never alone

# sisterhood

a prayer for one
blessed by four

deep connection

orchestrated by the one
far beyond the stars

brought together
to foster extension

a purpose

unveiled one by one

opening of hearts
sharing of minds

a sense of knowing
safety and home

each have a quality
a gift to share
completing the circle

generosity of heart
soul to soul
hand in hand
tall we stand

healing
courage
exploration
adventure

*we soar*

reaching deep into the soul
freeing the holds

our purpose flows

# a message
# (to niko & jake)

i text you

because i want you to know

no matter what is going on

in your life
in your mind
in your heart
in your soul

you are

lovable
worthy
capable

important and loved to the core

never settle for anything less
unconditional love and complete respect
hold on to a deep knowing in your soul you are
never ever alone

# innocence

of your own time and space

unworldly

a smile shining brilliance

unsullied

beautiful and sincere

unable to miss easy way gentle bliss

tenderness

not blocked by negativity or insolence

wildly free

composed of understanding compassion
and empathy

trusting

no compulsion to deceive or impress
but billowing with honesty integrity
morality and decency

# wind

i feel the wind on my face caressing
my body swaying

a lullaby

a calming rustling of the leaves
trees moving in symphony
waves of cleansing energy

closing my eyes i lean in
the strength of the wind holding me

free as a bird
i let go as it carries my wounded soul

# sunrise

a new day brings hope

casting a warm glow
as my heart becomes whole
i am emotional

grateful for a glimmer
a glorious sign of trust
knowing i can count on the sun
to rise no matter what

a glimpse of the sunrise
awakens my senses
a feeling of connection
to something sweeter
than my stressors

inspiring in me courage
to rise into my strength
trusting i am guided
and protected without exception

# tranquility

sandwiched between
two dark energies

eyelids closing
separating shielding

breathing in light
flushing through my body

expanding and drawing me up
light surrounding
filling me with serenity

dark energies evaporate

freedom from disturbance

tranquility

# God

light streaming down on me
like sunshine from above
consumes me with a knowing
that i am protected and loved

light energy radiating from within
a shield blocking forces
that try to penetrate my zen

a power like no other
allowing me to flourish

a sense of peace and calm
available to me every time i call
sending angels to catch me when i fall

a perfect love available to all

# filling from
# an empty cup

is it possible to build from emptiness

laying a foundation seems necessary
for success

nurturing my faith healing my soul
piece by piece completes the puzzle

granting myself space for reflection
and introspection leads me to growth

i am healing decades
of deep emotional pain and neglect
it is necessary to let each layer heal fully

massaging the salve
deep into the wounds
slows the bleeding

i find myself breathing more deeply
as i gaze toward the stars
there lie the answers
to questions unanswered

i remind myself
this is a sacred season
time is not important it is sufficient

# voices

i carry voices in my head
the things they have said

spoken by shadows

a reflection they see mirrored in me
something they are longing to be

they are just voices in my head
they cannot hurt me again

wisdom speaks from the intricate tapestry
of my soul

it is likely i have learned this lesson before

i imagine the wind carrying the voices
to their origin

so as not to unravel the delicate weave
of my heart soul and spirit

the moon and the stars know who i am

i will lean on them for reflection

i am nurturing a delicate balance
of heart soul and spirit as i discover
self-trust grounded in eloquence

# vibrational energy

those of us with a sentient soul
have been given a gift
a beautiful burden
feeling so deeply

a heart heavily laden with emotion
a heightened perception
we feel and we see
things no one else does

it can be confusing maddening
many times people do not believe you

a gift that comes with tremendous
responsibility
learning to harness it can be daunting

susceptible to absorbing
what we are not responsible for
can be disadvantageous
and even dangerous

especially when you get drawn into
a funnel of negative or dark energy

return the energy gently
with compassion and respect
allowing the owners to deal
with a consequence
an opportunity to reflect

with hope they take the chance
to heal what is causing them
to drain innocent souls that find
themselves in their destructive path

the energy and responsibility
belongs to them give it back
there is power in discerning

create confidence in yourself
and what you believe in

heal the parts of you
that have been ignored

there you will uncover wisdom
that will keep you steady
in your intuition and conviction

strengthening your foundation
to rise up to the calling
you have been given

a lightworker needed
to raise the black curtain

# patience a virtue

my scars will fade
my memories will stay
i get to pick and choose
how to file them away

moment by moment
i exercised tremendous patience
for that God has blessed me
the war is finally finished

the past is passed
i have no regrets
through this experience
my soul was made whole

i have awakened
i am flying free from the shadows
that were cast upon me

i will forever bask
in the delight that is freedom
grateful for the joy awaiting me

# acknowledgments

To those who shared love, who compassionately held space for me, who saw me and guided me to see myself, to those who came before me and chose to lead me to empowerment—I am overwhelmed with gratitude, I owe my healing to you.

May we always empower one another.

# about the author

When she's not writing poetry, Tami Hasapopoulos—
an integrative health and wellness practitioner with
a background in art and design—enjoys working with
creatives to unlock their potential through health and
wellness.

join me at
circle of wellness—
roots to healing

*Jami Hasapopallog*

I teach you how to use whole foods to target and heal symptoms as well as illnesses that inhibit your body's freedom. We will uncover the root cause of your disease. Learn how to combine delicious healing meals that are powerful, effective, and tailored to fit within *your* lifestyle. We will also explore protocols and tools that enhance your overall health and wellness.

*Looking for health freedom?*

I offer one-on-one coaching and six live virtual four-week teaching experiences:

- Holy Four (Wild Foods, Fruits, Vegetables, and Herbs & Spices)
- Morning Cleanse
- Sacred Sleep
- Truth about Caffeine
- Soul Healing
- Protein Fat and Healing

To learn more, visit circleofwellnessroots.com